DUDLEY SCHOOLS LIBRARY
AND INFORMATION SERVICE

KU-113-124

BLAME YOUR PARENTS

Buffy Silverman

Raintree

Schools Library and Infomation Services

S00000694332

www.raintreepublishers.co.uk
Visit our website to find out more information about Raintree books.

To order:
☎ Phone 44 (0) 1865 888112
🖹 Send a fax to 44 (0) 1865 314091
🖥 Visit the Raintree Bookshop at www.raintreepublishers.co.uk to browse our catalogue and order online.

First published in Great Britain by Raintree, Halley Court, Jordan Hill, Oxford OX2 8EJ, part of Harcourt Education.

Raintree is a registered trademark of Harcourt Education Ltd.

© Harcourt Education Ltd 2008
First published in paperback 2008
The moral right of the proprietor has been asserted.

All rights reserved. No part of this publication may be reproduced, stored in a retrieval system, or transmitted in any form or by any means, electronic, mechanical, photocopying, recording, or otherwise, without either the prior written permission of the publishers or a licence permitting restricted copying in the United Kingdom issued by the Copyright Licensing Agency Ltd, 90 Tottenham Court Road, London W1T 4LP (www.cla.co.uk).

Editorial: Nancy Dickmann and Catherine Veitch
Design: Philippa Jenkins and Q2A Creative
Illustrations: Peter Geissler
Picture Research: Hannah Taylor
Production: Alison Parsons

Originated by Modern Age
Printed and bound in China by Leo Paper Group

ISBN 978 1 4062 0732 3 (hardback)
12 11 10 09 08
10 9 8 7 6 5 4 3 2 1

ISBN 978 1 4062 0746 0 (paperback)
12 11 10 09 08
10 9 8 7 6 5 4 3 2 1

British Library Cataloguing in Publication Data
Silverman, Buffy
Blame your parents. – (Fusion)
576.5
A full catalogue record for this book is available from the British Library

Acknowledgements
The author and publisher are grateful to the following for permission to reproduce copyright material: Alamy p.**16** (Danita Delimont); Corbis pp.**18-19** (Annie Engel/zefa), **7** (Ralph A. Clevenger), **24** (Royalty-Free), **4-5** (Tom and Dee Ann McCarthy), **23** (Tom Stewart/zefa); FLPA p.**25** (David Hosking), **27** (Nigel Cattlin); NHPA pp.**8-9** (Stephen Dalton); Photolibrary.com p.**21** (Animals Animals/Earth Scenes), **14** (Botanica), **20** (Phototake Inc), **6** (Wendy Shattil & Bob Rozinski/Oxford Scientific), **12-13** (Workbook, Inc); Science Photo Library pp.**10-11** (Prof. K.Seddon and Dr. T.Evans, Queen's University Belfast).

Cover photograph of various images to form a counterfit face reproduced with permission of Corbis (Lucidio Studio Inc, Serge Krouglikoff); photos.com.

The publishers would like to thank Nancy Harris and Harold Pratt for their assistance in the preparation of this book.

Every effort has been made to contact copyright holders of any material reproduced in this book. Any omissions will be rectified in subsequent printings if notice is given to the publishers.

Disclaimer
All the Internet addresses (URLs) given in this book were valid at the time of going to press. However, due to the dynamic nature of the Internet, some addresses may have changed, or sites may have changed or ceased to exist since publication. While the author and publishers regret any inconvenience this may cause readers, no responsibility for any such changes can be accepted by either the author or the publishers.

It is recommended that adults supervise children on the Internet.

DUDLEY PUBLIC LIBRARIES

L ▪ ▪▪ ▪▪

694332   SCH

JS75.1

Contents

Some words are printed in bold, **like this**. You can find out what they mean on page 30. You can also look in the box at the bottom of the page where they first appear.

Blame your parents?

At the park many families gather for a picnic. Look at the children and at the adults. Which child belongs to which parent? How can you tell?

inherit receive a trait from a parent
trait physical or personality feature

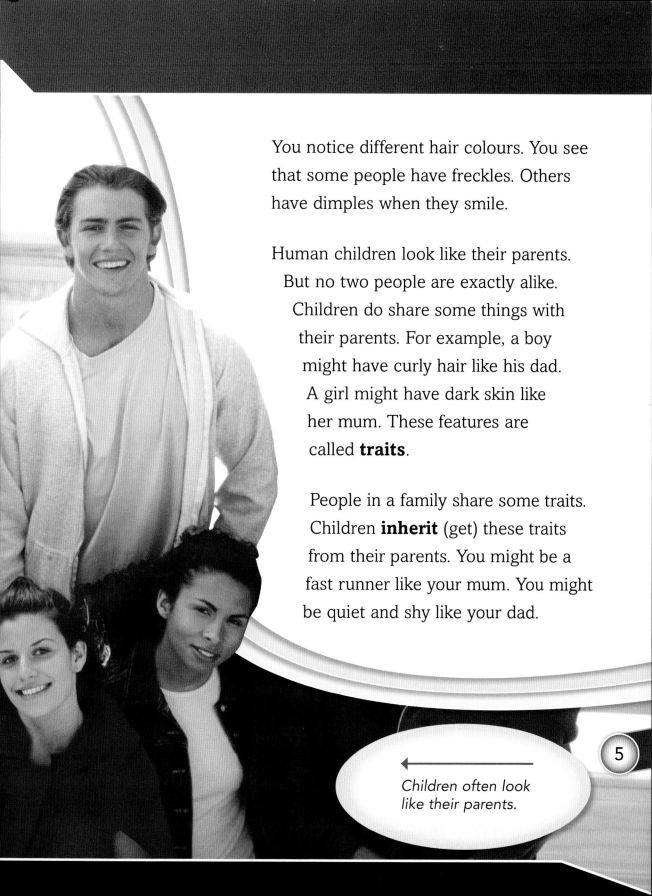

You notice different hair colours. You see that some people have freckles. Others have dimples when they smile.

Human children look like their parents. But no two people are exactly alike. Children do share some things with their parents. For example, a boy might have curly hair like his dad. A girl might have dark skin like her mum. These features are called **traits**.

People in a family share some traits. Children **inherit** (get) these traits from their parents. You might be a fast runner like your mum. You might be quiet and shy like your dad.

Children often look like their parents.

Animals and plants

In a park you see animal families. Young animals look like their parents. Young squirrels leap after their mother. They reach for acorns. They chew the acorns like their mother. Ducks swim after their parents. They paddle with their feet like their parents. Beech seeds drop from a beech tree. The seeds sprout. The new trees grow beech leaves like their parents.

These ducklings will grow up to look like their parents.

6

A caterpillar will grow up to look like its parents. This happens when it changes into a butterfly.

Changing shapes

Some insects look different at different stages of their lives. A monarch butterfly lays eggs. Caterpillars hatch from the eggs. The caterpillars look different from the monarch butterfly. These caterpillars then turn into butterflies. Now, they look like their butterfly parents.

Animal and plant **offspring** (children) look like their parents. Puppies grow into dogs, not cats. An acorn from an oak tree grows into an oak tree. It does not grow into a pine tree.

Thank your parents!

Take a look at animals around you. A squirrel leaps across tree branches. It has four legs and a long tail. It uses its legs to climb trees. Its tail helps it balance.

You cannot jump from branch to branch. But a squirrel cannot catch a ball like you can. It does not have long arms. It does not have hands that grasp.

You use all parts of your body to play sport. With your legs you race down the field. Your arms swing at your sides. Your hands grab a ball. Your eyes watch the ball. Your brain understands the rules of the sport.

All animals and plants have special **traits** (features). This squirrel **inherited** (got) its traits from its parents.

Why are you able to play sport? Thank your parents! You have two long legs, like your parents. You can walk or run, like your parents. Your hands can swing a bat. Your eyes let you focus on the action. You use your brain to understand.

In your genes

Why do children look like their parents? Your body has instructions that tell you how to grow. These instructions are called **genes**. Genes are made of a material called DNA. DNA is a code. It tells your body how to grow.

You read instructions when you build a model. Your body reads instructions in the same way. Your genes are the instructions.

Children **inherit** (get) genes from their parents. There are two genes for every **trait** (feature). One gene came from your mother. The other came from your father. You look like your parents because your genes came from them.

Living things are made of **cells**. Cells are the smallest part of a living thing. You are made of millions of cells. Every cell has a copy of your genes.

cell smallest unit of a living thing
gene set of instructions that tell a living thing how to grow

This is a model of DNA. Real DNA is much too small to see.

Gene count

People have over 30,000 genes in each cell. A fruit fly only has about 13,000 genes.

Furry genes

Genes are a mixture of two sets of instructions.
One set of genes comes from the mother.
The other is from the father.

Dogs have different kinds of fur. Genes tell them which fur to grow.

12

dominant form of gene that always causes a trait
recessive form of gene that requires two copies to cause a trait

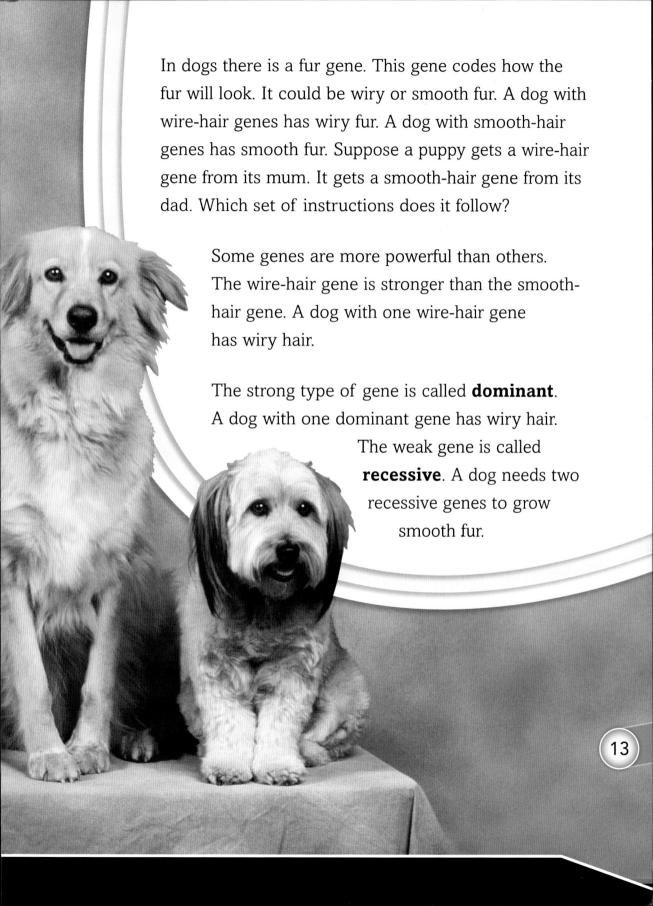

In dogs there is a fur gene. This gene codes how the fur will look. It could be wiry or smooth fur. A dog with wire-hair genes has wiry fur. A dog with smooth-hair genes has smooth fur. Suppose a puppy gets a wire-hair gene from its mum. It gets a smooth-hair gene from its dad. Which set of instructions does it follow?

Some genes are more powerful than others. The wire-hair gene is stronger than the smooth-hair gene. A dog with one wire-hair gene has wiry hair.

The strong type of gene is called **dominant**. A dog with one dominant gene has wiry hair. The weak gene is called **recessive**. A dog needs two recessive genes to grow smooth fur.

13

Red or white?

Plants have **genes**, just like animals. Genes tell plants how to grow. They tell a plant what colour flower to make.

Pea plants can grow red or white flowers. They **inherit** (get) a gene for flower colour from each parent. These genes tell a pea plant which colour flower to grow.

The gene for red flowers is the **dominant** (stronger) one. A plant with at least one dominant gene for flower colour grows red flowers. The gene for white flowers is the **recessive** (weaker) one. A plant with white flowers got white genes from both parents.

Discovery!

Gregor Mendel wondered how plants inherit **traits** (features). He grew thousands of pea plants. Some had round peas. Some had wrinkled peas. He studied his plants. He decided that each trait had two forms. One form was dominant. One form was recessive.

↑ Genes code for red or white flowers in pea plants.

Genes for pea plant flower colour

key
R = gene for red flower colour
r = gene for white flower colour

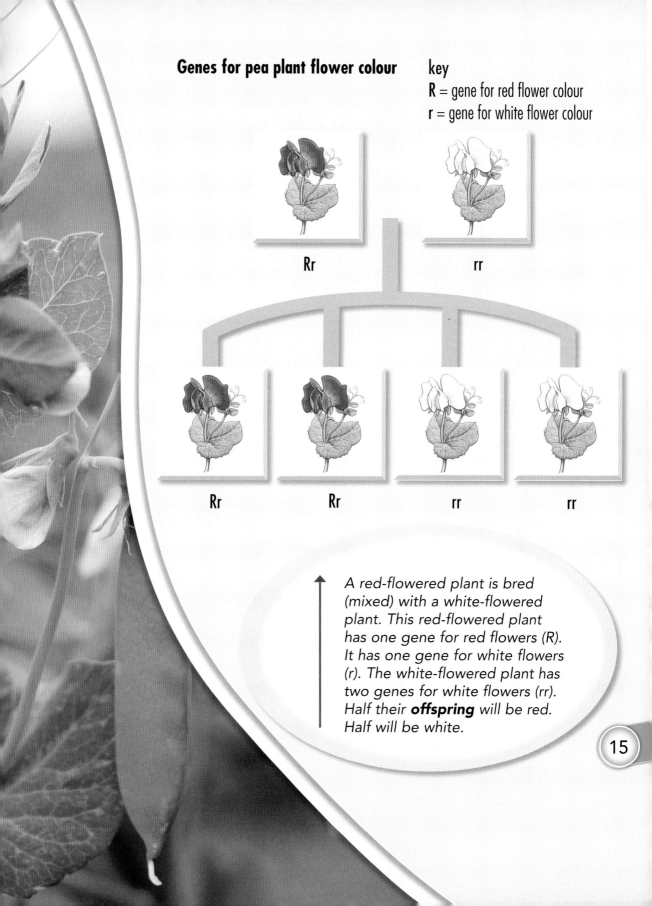

Rr   rr

Rr   Rr   rr   rr

*A red-flowered plant is bred (mixed) with a white-flowered plant. This red-flowered plant has one gene for red flowers (R). It has one gene for white flowers (r). The white-flowered plant has two genes for white flowers (rr). Half their **offspring** will be red. Half will be white.*

Freckled faces

Sometimes a child has a **trait** that is different from the child's parents. Two parents have freckled faces. But their child has no freckles. How can that be?

A pair of **genes** codes for freckles. The gene that codes for freckles is the **dominant** (stronger) one. If even one of the pair is the freckle gene, the person will have freckles. The other gene might be the weaker, or **recessive**, gene. The recessive gene codes for no freckles.

You inherit (get) freckles from your parents.

A parent with freckles must have one freckle gene. The other gene could be the freckle or non-freckle gene. Suppose both parents have one freckle and one non-freckle gene. Their child can **inherit** (get) two non-freckle genes. The child will not have freckles.

Freckle fact

The amount of time a person spends in the Sun can change his or her freckles. Sunlight makes freckles get darker.

One child has no freckles. His parents do have freckles. He has inherited two non-freckle (recessive) genes.

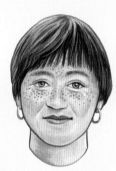

Genes for freckles

key
F = gene for freckles
f = gene for no freckles

F

f

F

FF

Ff

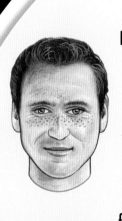

f

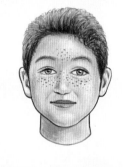

Ff

ff

17

Seeing double

Children in a family do not look exactly the same. That is because they have different **genes**. Brothers and sisters do not get the same mix of genes from their parents.

But **identical twins** look almost exactly alike. They look alike because they have identical genes. Identical twins start from one **cell**. A cell is the smallest unit of a living thing. That cell splits and makes more cells. All the cells have the same genes. Both twins get the same genes.

Identical twins look alike. This is because they have the same genes.

identical twins   set of twins with the same genes

Identical twins are the only people who have exactly the same genes. Because they have the same genes, they are always the same sex. Two girls may be identical twins. Two boys may be identical twins. But a boy and a girl cannot be identical twins.

Carbon copy

Not all living things with identical **genes** are twins. A parent and **offspring** (child) can also have identical genes. Normally it takes two parents to make a child. The child gets a mix of both parents' genes. But sometimes a living thing grows from one parent. Then, the offspring gets an exact copy of the parent's genes.

Sometimes a living thing makes an identical copy of itself. This copy is called a **clone**. A clone has the same genes as its parent. Many plants make identical copies of themselves. A strawberry plant grows long stems called runners. New plants grow on runners. These plants are clones of their parent. They have the same genes as the parent strawberry plant.

Dolly the sheep lived for six years.

clone individual or cell with identical genes to its parent

Strawberry plants grow clones on their runners. ↓

Cell cloning

Scientists want to cure diseases with cloning. They hope to clone healthy **cells** for ill people. Cells are the smallest units of a living thing. The healthy cells might help ill people get well.

Scientists can clone animals. They have cloned sheep. Dolly was the first cloned sheep. Dolly had the same genes as her mother.

Genes and learning

Even **identical twins** are not *exactly* alike. One twin might play football better than the other. One twin might play the violin better. Their **genes** are exactly alike. Why are the twins different?

People can learn different skills. When you practise a skill, you become better at it. Through practice, you learn new things.

If you join a football team, you practise running and kicking. You learn to be a better player. You might have genes that code for long legs. You might have genes that help you run fast. But you will not learn to play without practice.

When you were younger, you learned the letters of the alphabet. Then, you learned to read. With practice, you become a better reader. The genes that you got from your parents did not tell you how to read. Reading is a skill that you learn through practice.

This girl's long legs help her on the football field. But she must also practise how to score a goal.

Tall tales

You might be taller than some friends. You might be shorter than others. If your parents are short, you probably will be short. **Genes** play a part in height.

But even with "tall" genes, a person might not grow tall. People need to eat food to grow. They need to stay healthy. Without good food, people do not grow as tall.

↑ Genes make people tall or short.

In many countries people eat more food today than in the past. They are ill less often. Because of medicines, children do not stay ill.

People today are taller than in the past. Today, British men are taller. They are almost 8 centimetres (3 inches) taller than they were 100 years ago. Dutch people are the tallest in the world. Their genes and their healthy diet make them grow tall.

A flamingo's feather colour depends on its genes. It also depends on its food. Flamingos eat pink shrimp. The colour in shrimp makes their feathers grow a deeper pink.

Green giants

Plants grow to different sizes. **Genes** play a part in how big a plant grows. An oak tree grows taller than a dandelion. That is because it has different instructions in its genes.

Genes can tell plants how tall to grow. But plants also need water and good soil to grow. They make more leaves if they get what they need. A plant's **environment** (surroundings) can change how tall it grows.

The environment can also harm a plant. Wind and ice damage plants. In a storm, tree branches fall and stems break. A plant that is damaged does not grow as tall.

Bad taste

Many insects chew plant leaves. Genes let some plants fight back! Caterpillars chew radish leaves. When caterpillars chew, the radish plant makes a bad-tasting substance. Insects will not eat these bad-tasting leaves. A gene tells the plant to make the bad-tasting substance. The gene does not work until the leaves are chewed.

environment plant's or animal's surroundings

Plants grow taller when they get what they need. ↑

Whom should you blame?

Your **genes** told your ears how to grow! There are different types of earlobe. Some people have earlobes that hang down. Others have earlobes attached to their head. One pair of genes determines how earlobes grow.

The gene for free-hanging earlobes is **dominant** (stronger). A person with at least one dominant gene has free-hanging earlobes. The gene for attached earlobes is **recessive**. It is the weaker form of the gene. A person with attached earlobes has two recessive genes.

Look in a mirror. What type of earlobe do you have? Are your earlobes free-hanging? If so, you have at least one dominant gene. Or are your lobes attached? Then you have two recessive genes.

Check your family's earlobes. What type of earlobe do they have? Look at the earlobes of each member of your family. Decide which genes each person has.

Whom should you blame?

Genes for earlobes

key
F = gene for free-hanging earlobes
f = gene for attached earlobes

F f

F

f

FF Ff

Ff ff

We get earlobe genes from our parents.

Glossary

cell smallest unit of a living thing. Our bodies are made of cells.

clone individual or cell with identical genes to its parent. Strawberry plants grow new plants that are clones.

dominant form of gene that always causes a trait. A pea plant with one or two dominant genes for red flower colour grows red flowers. Red is the dominant gene for pea plant flower colour.

environment plant's or animal's surroundings. A plant grows taller if there is enough water and good soil in its environment.

gene set of instructions that tell a living thing how to grow. Living things have genes in every cell of the body.

identical twins set of twins with the same genes. Identical twins look alike.

inherit receive a trait from a parent. Children can inherit dimples from their parents.

offspring child of a person, animal, or plant. Parents pass on their genes to their offspring.

recessive form of gene that requires two copies to cause a trait. A pea plant with two recessive genes for white flower colour grows white flowers. White is the recessive gene for pea plant flower colour.

trait physical or personality feature. Height and eye colour are two physical human traits. Being shy or confident are personality traits.

Want to know more?

Books to read

- *Have a Nice DNA*, Frances R. Balkwill (Cold Spring Harbor Laboratory, 2002)

- *Baa! The Most Interesting Book You'll Ever Read About Genes and Cloning*, Cynthia Pratt Nicolson (Kids Can, 2001)

- *From Egg to Adult*, Mike Unwin (Heinemann Library, 2004)

Websites

- www.sciencemuseum.org.uk/exhibitions/genes/index.asp
  This guide to genetics looks at genes and how they work.
- www.ology.amnh.org/genetics/index.html
  Go on a genetic journey. Take part in fun quizzes and find out about what makes you who you are.

Read more about animals and their offspring in *Does a Worm Have a Girlfriend?*

Some animals have babies in unusual ways! Find out more in *Animal Secrets*.

Index